21ˢᵗ Century Leadership Guides

I0170120

Solving Problems

A Guide To Being a Person of Impact

Dr. Ed Brenegar

An Imprint of Circle of Impact Press

21st Century Leadership Guides

An Imprint of Circle of Impact Press

May Your No Be A Yes:

A Guide To Making Better Decisions

©2021 by Dr. Ed Brenegar All Rights Reserved

ISBN (ebook): 978-1-7373097-2-7

ISBN (print): 978-1-7373097-3-4

Circle of Impact Press

North Wilkesboro, North Carolina

Published in the United States

Dedication

Tom Campbell
President

Black Mountain Home for Children,
Youth, and Families
Black Mountain, North Carolina

A Visionary Leader of the First Order

Contents

Chapter One:
The Solution is Impact

It is the most human thing to take a problem and try to solve it. As a child, I built model cars, planes, and ships. I'd open the box and there before me were all these little plastic pieces. I

would read through the assembly page and then start. The chaos in the box was a promise that order could be created in the form of a B-29 World War Two era bomber like the one my father flew in during the war. The focus, the initial frustration, and the trial and error of learning how to solve the problem of the mess in the box led to a genuine sense of accomplishment. I've been solving problems ever since.

Even my children noticed. My oldest son, when he was ten, told an adult who asked him what his father did, said: "Dad talks people into having problems and offers to fix them." Yes!

Precisely right.

One of my fondest childhood memories of my father was the year that we spent assembling a short-wave radio. Usually Sunday afternoons, we'd go upstairs to my parent's bedroom where on the family's card table were all the components. Step by step we'd solder connections.

Never knowing, always hoping, that we had done it correctly. When we were done, we plugged the radio in, turned it on, and magically, we picked up the BBC World Service. To solve the problem of assembly, the final outcome was always on our mind.

When I am writing, I go to bed early, wake up after a few hours of sleep, and go sit at my desk to write for an hour or so, then return to bed. It is a regular pattern for me. One night after finishing the first draft of this book, I woke up realizing that my book on problem-solving had become a problem. Something was missing.

Many times as a child building a model car the same thing happened. I'd end up with extra parts. The problem with assembly was that I ignored parts that didn't make sense. As a result, the model was never complete, never perfect. I've heard artists say a book, a painting, or a film is never complete, just abandoned. I wasn't ready to do that. Because the problem of the book was not the book, but me. My own perception was far more limited than I actually knew when I sat down to write.

There were two things missing. One was a description of different ways to solve problems. The other was a description of who we are as people who are problem solvers.

What was missing? The joy of problem-solving. The creative process of problem-solving. I was so wrapped up in trying to help people find ways to solve their problems, I forget about why.

What follows is a book on the creative process of problem-solving. The book in your hand or illuminated on your device is the product of the solution that I sought in writing. May all your problems find solutions, and may your solutions bring joy and satisfaction.

Why We Solve Problems

The awareness begins with an impression or a comment by someone. In that moment, we know that there is a problem. How do we know? Something isn't quite right. Something is missing, out-of-kilter, misaligned, or simply, broken. We listen for the logic of some appeal or argument and it doesn't make sense. If you are aware, you will see problems. This is not a negative thing. It means you can see the world beyond the surface of things. You can see both the wholeness of the world and its brokenness. Seeing the latter and knowing the former places us in a position to be people of impact.

Being aware is where this creative process begins. We are aware of the parts that aren't fitting or are missing. The question is "Do we want to solve this problem?" Our awareness is not just about the problem. We see the context. We see why it is a problem. We see the impact of the problem. This awareness is a real power to make a difference.

People who are unaware are dependent on other people and institutions to do for them what they will not do for themselves. Are they unaware because they choose to ignore the problems occurring right in front of them? They don't want to see problems. Like the proverbial ostrich, they stick their head in the sand hoping the problem will go away. It is a fearful way to live.

Always dependent, hoping that people and institutions have their best interests in mind.

This is a reason why people are resistant to change. Without awareness and the willingness to solve problems, fear and a lack of self-confidence can come to dominate our lives. We begin to look for people to blame for our problems. Each step in this direction magnifies each problem we face.

If this is where you are. If you are living in fear. If you are afraid of breaking some rule. If you are unsure about who you are, and what your future life is going to be. Then, you need to begin to solve the problems that have walled you in from the life of impact that is waiting to be realized.

Impact is a change that makes a difference that matters. Impact comes from solving problems. Solving problems is creating change. The change in us is a clearer perspective, greater self- confidence in facing the challenges that come with life.

My friend Emmanuel is a pastor of a church in a poor community near Kampala, Uganda. When his country was locked down because of the global pandemic, he asked me what he should do. The people in his community were hungry. Some were starving. I suggested that he go to his local elected officials and tell them that if they got the food, he would distribute it. He did and together they fed their people.

Was the problem solved? No. It was a one-time arrangement. As the saying goes, "Give a man a fish and he eats for a day. Teach a man to fish and he eats for a lifetime."

Knowing this, Emmanuel rented land. Planted maize in early summer and with a crew of helpers harvested food for his people. He is now looking at a new, larger tract of land to rent. Now the problem is where to find the equipment to farm it. The pastor became a farmer because his people were hungry. He took responsibility to solve their problem in a creative way. He is now moving to the next level of solution.

We solve problems because we can. It is part awareness, part creativity, and part being a person of responsibility. It is a solution to a life of fear and dependence.

Not far from where Emmanuel lives, across the border in Kenya, a group of forty-five women are in a program learning to farm. They came together to meet me and talk about what they were learning. They begin with one chicken, advance to vegetable gardens, dairy cows, and, ultimately, forestry as they acquire land.

As I interviewed them, they talked about taking responsibility for the welfare of their families. Their goal in solving this problem through farming was to be self-sufficient and interdependent. By learning to farm, they were learning to not be dependent and live in fear of the crime that comes with idleness.

On that day, these poor women from a rural corner of Africa became my teachers. Through them, I could see problems that I had avoided that because I reasoned, I had more important things to do. A link to my interview with them can be found in the resources section at the end of the book. If you feel that your life is not self-sufficient and interdependent with your family and neighbors, then you have a problem that you can begin to address.

Chapter Two:
The Global Impact of
Solving Problems

The same desire resides in those who seek to discover cures for cancer or extreme poverty. The problems can be larger and more complex marshalling all our capacities of body, mind, and spirit.

This picture is of twenty-nine scientists who attended the Solvay Conference on Physics in Brussels, Belgium in 1927. Seventeen of them would become Nobel prize winners. Think of them as the Physics Hall of Fame of the 20th century. In their circle is Albert Einstein (first row, fifth from the left), Madame Marie Curie (the only woman participant), Niels Bohr (second row, farthest to the right), Max Planck (first row, seated at Madame Curies right), Paul Dirac (second row, fifth from the left), Werner Eisenberg (third row, ninth from the left), and Erwin Shrödinger (third row, sixth from the left). There

are links to their bios in the resources section at the end of the book. Every one of these scientists were problem solvers. They are the scientists who developed quantum theory that open to us the nuclear age.

We know them today because of the solutions that they brought to their fields of science. They didn't begin as the great men and women of science. They were people working in obscurity.

Through their research, they became aware of the problems of knowledge and science. They labored hard. Many with insufficient support until their discoveries brought them recognition and honor.

Einstein wrote his three most important papers on the physics of relativity while working at the Swiss patent office. Madame Curie's, a Polish émigré to France, earliest laboratory was nothing more than a small shack. She also had to overcome cultural obstacles to become the first woman to receive a Nobel prize. Look again at that picture. Seventeen Nobel prize winners.

Marie Curie is the only won awarded twice, and for two different fields, physics and chemistry. None of them started out as Nobel laureates. They were like all of us. People seeking answers to questions that we have. They are our predecessors in problem-solving.

We don't wake up one morning and say, "I going to solve problems today!" Most likely we lay in bed, awake in the middle of the night, wrestling with a question that we have to solve. It has to be solved so we can take care of the responsibilities of life, family, and work.

In my conversations with people, this is what they tell me. They see problems at their work or in their families. It bothers them. Something though stands in the way of solving it. These gentlemen and one woman, Madame Marie Curie, also faced obstacles to their problem- solving. They forged ahead treating every obstacle as a problem to solve.

They found out, as I believe we can too, how important it is that we need each other to solve the problems that we face. The problems that I want to solve, of human purpose for impact, can't be done just by writing books. The problem of human initiative must be solved collaboratively in action. This is why Emmanuel and I are in constant communication about how he and the people from his church can solve the problems of poverty in their community. As we have regularly talked, others are beginning to join in. A network of problem solvers is growing.

We solve problems because we must. It is how we live our lives. In every decision, every game we play, every project we begin, every conversation we have, we are solving problems. Look at the Circle of Impact below. It is a guide for solving problems. Not just some, but all of our problems. The Circle of Impact is how we can learn to be aware. Even the awareness of why we are afraid, why we are dependent upon people and structures that do not have our best interest at heart.

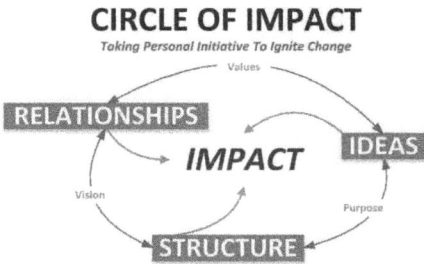

CIRCLE OF IMPACT
Taking Personal Initiative To Ignite Change

Values

RELATIONSHIPS

IMPACT   IDEAS

Vision   Purpose

STRUCTURE

Through this model, we can see how in every idea, every relationship, every social and organizational structure, problems come to be. We can also see that the path to a solution is through aligning the three dimensions for impact. If we could, then we find that the small problems that we face each day can be resolved, and we can move onto larger problems like those that Emmanuel is addressing in his community.

When you become a problem solver, you become a person of impact. For every new problem you solve, some change that makes a difference that matters happens. You learn how to be a responsible person in your home, in your community, and for the world.

If we could find a way to believe that we, each of us as individuals, can be a person whose problem solving impacts the world, then problems that we once thought of unsolvable, could be solved in a minute or two. The process of problem solving follows our awareness and belief that we can be people who make a difference that matters.

Chapter Three:
Hidden Potential for
Problem Solving

One of the principles behind my belief in problem solving has to do with the nature of leadership. Not the leadership of organizations, though that does factor in, but the leadership of our lives. My varied experience with people showed me that all leadership begins with personal initiative to create impact that makes a difference that matters. I saw and benefited from people who saw problems and fixed them. As a result, I have grown to be able to see the potential in people for making a difference in their life.

Early in my career, I would ask people about what their potential could be. I'd ask

organizational leaders what they thought was the potential of their people. Many didn't understand what

I was talking about. They simply thought living was about getting what you can out of a situation. This is not what I see as potential.

Potential is the range of difference that we can make over the course of our lives. Few people think in these terms. They don't see themselves as persons of potential. Who do they see themselves to be? They don't know.

The modern world is not oriented towards fulfilling potential. It is rather designed for people to fit into institutional structures. As a result, there is no identity apart from participation in the collection of institutional structures that frame our lives.

There is a significant problem here. Human beings don't function well as robots. We are creative beings who see problems.

If you spend any time with social media, you will find a lot of very angry, bitter, extraordinarily critical people complaining about everything. Think about that for a moment. The simplest explanation for all these expressions is that these people have identified a problem. Yet, they don't believe that they are responsible for the problem or its solution. Who is? Someone else or some organization is responsible.

Can you see the human reality here? We are really good at identifying problems. Problems are everywhere. But we are not so good at solving them. Why is this? It is because we have been conditioned to act according to what we are told to do. Solving problems requires personal initiative. It demands us to think and be creative, and then act to resolve the problem.

The level of problem solving that many people do has the effect of also convincing them that they don't have much potential for making a difference.

When I have had conversations about this topic, we often end up talking about work. I ask them if they feel that they are fulfilling the potential that they bring to the job every day. They usually describe the various obstacles that make problem solving difficult.

On several occasions, I have asked the person if she thought her boss trusted her. The response is usually, "for the little things." The institutional structure of business often is the obstacle to greater productivity from employees. In this sense, structure is to people as water is to fish. We can't see it because it is an all-encompassing environment.

Defining Potential

Let's define potential as unlimited possibility. Given our talent, skills, experience, and relationships with people, there is an unlimited possibility for problem solving. If our talent, skills, experience, and the quality of our relationships grow, then our potential must grow as well.

If potential is unlimited for each of us, it doesn't mean that we can do anything we want. There is only one Albert Einstein, just as there is only one of you. Your impact and the outcome of

your use of talent, skills, experience, and relationships is unlimited. Yet, our potential doesn't exist as something complete now. We are not given a fixed amount to use throughout our life.

It doesn't come packaged in a box. "Here's your potential. Use it wisely." No. It is the exact opposite. The more potential you realize as impact the more your potential grows.

Think about the picture of the world-renown scientists above. Can you imagine Albert Einstein sitting at his desk in a room of other clerks filing patent applications? What do you think his co- workers thought? He's a kind of nerdy guy. His head's lost in the clouds. Could anyone have imagined that he would become one of the most important scientists of the 20th century? Let's take Marie Curie, the only woman in the picture, who was a pioneer in the discovery of radioactivity. What do you think her grade school teachers thought of her potential? "Oh, she's a bright child. She'll probably be a school teacher."

All of us have been underestimated for what is possible. It is difficult to look out to the future and imagine what realized potential looks like. For this reason, we look back at people like Einstein and Curie and think is my potential as unlimited as theirs? Yes, it is.

Let me be clear about what I am saying to you. No one at any point in your life can tell you what your potential is. No one. Not even yourself. It is unlimited because it grows as we grow.

We want to be able to look at the child and imagine their potential in life. Maybe they will do well in school or excel on the ball field. The reality is that there is no way to know the potential of a person when they are young because we do not know how willing the child will be to work hard to overcome all their limitations to excel at what they love to do.

We should look at a person's whole life and ask what do they need to excel at creating impact?

It isn't just good schooling. It is also good parenting. A good social culture with mentors and close friends. Potential is the measure of the whole life of a person. It isn't just what they produce for their employer or what they can accumulate from the financial compensation that they earn. Potential is more than all those.

We are all born with potential. Many people think it is a fixed amount. You can see it in our culture's attitude towards retirement. By the time we reach our mid-60s, our potential is spent. Used up. Done. Over. Gone. I know that this is a false representation of human potential. I am past the age that I should have retired. I am now in a new chapter of my life which promises to be the most impactful. The key to expanding your potential is to never get stuck simply repeating what you have done all your life. We must change in order for our real potential to manifest itself through the finish line of our life. As my high school track coach taught me, you run through the finish line, not to it.

There are people who are considered late bloomers who didn't make a dent in the world until after retirement age. One of the most influential business writers of the 20th century was Peter Drucker, known as The Father of Management. Thirty of his thirty-nine books were published after the age of sixty. Imagine people asking at your 60th birthday, "So, ready to retire yet?" Many of us will build our legacy of impact after everyone has finished their career.

The real problem of potential is how we define it. It is not an amount of contribution to be expended or things to acquire as a measure of success. It is, rather, our individual capacity for making a difference that matters. The measure of potential is change. What changes because of what you do in those activities? What changes about you because of the things you purchased as a sign of your status? Those things don't last.

Consider the potential for impact as something that grows. I like to think of our lives as growing through four timeframes. There is the past which was a time of learning. The present is a time for action. The future is a time where our impact is realized. The future may be tomorrow or the next decade. It is still that time that our past and present is preparing us to accomplish. All the decades of our lives are times for creating impact. The last timeframe is our legacy.

Our legacy is what remains after we are gone. There are only two things that last after we pass from this earth. One is our reputation; how we will be remembered. What is the impact that you want to be remembered for creating? The other legacy is the difference we made in our relationships. How did we impact the people in our lives? What difference did you make that changed their lives?

If we think of potential this way, then we realize that potential continues to grow or diminish throughout the whole of our life.

My own experience follows this trajectory. It is more like a story with chapters. Chapter one took me through childhood into the early stages of my career. When I discovered that leadership was my calling, chapter two began. Thirty-five years of research, practice, experimentation, and analysis culminating in the publication of Circle of Impact. After almost a year of traveling to promote the book, I realized that I had come to the end of this chapter, and a new one was beginning. As I sought to understand this transition, it became clear to me that all those years were a time of preparation for the work that will occupy the remainder of my life. Because chapter three required me to lay aside what I had been doing to begin a whole new work, it also meant that in that moment my potential expanded exponentially. How do I know this? In many respects, and people close to me may tell you this, that I spent all those years in my head, trying to understand the depths of leadership and organizations. The focus has now shifted to the support of networks of relationships around the world who are forming to care for their local communities. In this regard, I am now a trainer, a facilitator, a connector of people, and a believer in the potential of people to create impact far beyond their imagination.

Potential and Creativity

When I hear people talking about problem solving, it always sounds like something technical. I'll go into this aspect of problem solving later. It is a process that uses specific techniques to resolve the problem. However, just knowing the technical side of problem solving does address the human dimension of problem solving.

Human beings like puzzles and games. They challenge us to think through situations. Because they are games, the consequence of failing and starting over is minimal. It reminds me of the game Chip's Challenge that had all these levels to get through to the end of the game. I never did. But I kept trying. That is the point. The more you keep at the game, the more your creativity comes to matter.

Creativity is simply a process of taking the parts, like in my airplane model example above and doing something different with it. For example, many shows feature teams of car lovers customizing their cars. It is a highly creative process. Their purpose is to solve two problems. How do I make my car cooler than it was when it left the factory? How do I improve the performance? Both of those are problems that require creativity to solve. If it didn't require creativity, it wouldn't be any fun.

I hope you see where I am headed. Problem solving is not just about solving problems that negatively affect people and communities. It is also about creating the kind of place we really want to live in. When we take personal initiative to create impact, we are solving problems, and we are creating an environment that we want to live in.

If you have ever built a house, you will know what I mean. Every house has the basic components of bedrooms, bathrooms, kitchen, living spaces, and places for storage. If you are building a house, you are not going to settle for just rooms that are off the shelf of the home improvement center. You creatively build a house that will enable you to have the domestic home life that you desire. The problem is the construction of the house. The creativity is in developing and envisioning what it should be. And this creativity has everything to do with fulfilling the potential we have for the life we want to live.

We fulfill our potential through creativity solving our problems. However, before we can do this, we need to be clear about what matters to us. The solution to a problem begins as an idea about why something is a problem. We evaluate our lives by the values that matter to us. We all live by these values, even if we are unaware of what they are. Values are the foundation of understanding and belief about all aspects of our lives. As a result, we gain a sense of purpose that focuses on why certain problems are important and others are not. Our values also draw us towards certain people who can join in solving our problems. This is where our network of relationships come from. We share common values and a perception of the problems that we can solve together.

One of the outcomes of Emmanuel's efforts in Uganda to feed his people is a small network of himself, another pastor named James who works with orphans, and me. We share similar values about how problems in developing nations should be addressed. Our purpose is to build a network of people where they can find and develop the resources that they need to meet the needs of their communities.

Before we get to the techniques of problem solving, we see that it is a creative process drawing upon the full potential of our lives and the relationships that we have with people. Out of this perspective, I hope you see that to be a problem solving means that the impact of our lives will grow, creating a legacy that will last long after we have passed on.

Chapter Four: Thinking about Problem Solving

It is common to think that problem solving is primarily a thinking game. What we mean by thinking is worth exploring. Over the past hundred years, the world of thinking has transitioned from being primarily a philosophical subject to one about science. I am neither a trained scientist nor philosopher and suspect that most of you are not either. However, I am a keen observer of human behavior, both on the individual level and the group or organizational level. Ever since I was in college I looked to philosophers and scientists to discover insight into what I saw. The result is that I learned the value and limitation of thinking as a separate activity of our lives.

Let us frame this discussion in terms of different ways of thinking. I am going to describe these ways more metaphorically than literally. I will use the language that philosophers and scientists use to describe how their work represents ways that we can understand how to think more expansively to solve the myriad of problems that we face every day.

The Openness of the World

In the early 1930s, Austrian physicist Kurt Gödel discovered a principle in the field of mathematics that he called the "incompleteness" theory. He found that certain mathematical problems could be solved, but not consistently. His discovery shook the world of mathematics because scientists believed that consistency was "the sole criterion" determining the proof of a mathematical theory.

From my amateur perspective, this tells me that the world before us is always open to new ways of understanding. This idea is one of the reasons that I speak about transition so much. Life is not static. No answer to a problem is ever the final answer. There is always some new information emerging to cause us to rethink or respond to what we have seen before. It is why my Circle of Impact model incorporates questioning into the process. These questions, which I will introduce later, are intended to keep us open to our own discoveries. It is a way not to get stuck. There is always a way out of a problem that we face.

Long before Kurt Gödel discovered his "incompleteness" theory, the world of philosophy impacted our world during a time called the Age of Enlightenment. In many respects, these thinkers constructed ways of thinking that are still with us today. French philosopher and mathematician Rene' Descartes was one of these philosophers who changed the world. He did so with a simple statement. He presented it in Latin as "cogito, ergo sum", and we translate this into the famous phrase, "I think, therefore I am." Underlying this statement is an experience we have when we ask questions. We can answer our questions because we think about them. If I am thinking, then I exist. I am alive. All this may seem very obvious to us who don't live in our heads every day. However, for philosophers and scientists, it was an important affirmation of what it means to be a human being.

However, we are not just thinking beings. We just don't ask questions to solve problems in our minds. We want solutions that lead to action. We want to learn from the practical aspects of solving problems. About a decade ago, I was introduced to the thoughts of French philosopher Maurice Merleau-Ponty. He wrote a massive book called The Phenomenology of Perception.

For our purposes, what is important is his perspective on perception. Think of perception as awareness. Ever drive down a busy street and you have an intuition that you need to slow down or even stop?

This has happened to me once. It was before dawn on my birthday in June. I left my home in Jackson, Wyoming headed north to spend the day hiking in Yellowstone National Park. The drive there takes me through Grand Teton National Park. I was driving at about twenty-five miles-per-hour through the park, the light of dawn was just breaking. All of a sudden I had the feeling that I needed to stop. As I did, I looked twenty feet in front of me, and there standing across the road was a massive bull Bison. If I had not stopped, I would have driven under his belly, between his front and rear legs, and he would have rolled up over my car, crushing me. I still shudder when I think of that moment.

My awareness to stop came from my perception of my surroundings. I realized that I saw something that I had not consciously seen. We see with our eyes. We hear with our ears. We taste with our mouths. We smell with our noses. We feel with our skin. Each of these senses provides us information that gives us a notion of something going on.

This is how we perceive or understand the world. We think in order to make sense of what we perceive. In other words, we are not just thinking beings or sensing beings, we are whole beings. We are healthiest when all parts of our lives are working together aligned for awareness and understanding. Solving problems is one way we bring all these aspects of our lives together for meaning and impact.

For example, realtors know that if you put a pot of spiced tea on the stove or burn a cinnamon candle during an open house that it connects the house to memories of home. When we walk out the door in the morning, we can tell what the weather will be without looking at an app. We can tell there is more moisture in the air and it is warmer than yesterday. It is also the case that even while asleep, a parent's ears are tuned to their baby's sounds. The other day I opened the door of my home and I smelled hot rubber. I knew something was burning. Quickly, I found a hot electrical outlet. If I had not smelled it, a fire would certainly have started.

We are human beings who not only think about the world but also perceive it through our senses. We learn to be cautious when we smell fire, hear a child's cry, see a glass about to fall off a table, touch a hot pot on the stove, and taste food that is spoiled. We experience the world through our senses. We learn to understand the world that we experience by asking questions that help us make sense of what we experience. The more we are connected to the physical world, the greater the opportunities of learning about how the world functions. As a child, a long time ago, one of my teachers told our class that "experience is the best teacher." Since we learn this way, how do we learn to think from life's experience?

Two Kinds of Thinking

I have been asking questions about thinking and problem solving for as long as I can remember. Early on I came across Michael Polanyi, a Hungarian physicist and philosopher, who wrote about what he calls tacit knowledge. Polanyi showed how we operate in our lives based on knowledge that we are not conscious of at the moment we are utilizing it. We use tacit knowledge when we write with pen and paper. It is how we can drive a car, or type words into a document like I am right now. We learn to read by first learning letters, then words, then strings of words called sentences. If we were to always read in that sequence of letters, words, and then sentences, we would never learn what those structures point to, which is information and knowledge. We read with tacit knowledge. It is sub-conscious learning that is a learned skill that we all have.

Polanyi represents a generation of scientists/philosophers that followed Gödel's time. He said that we know more than we can tell. We do because we learn from personal experience. When we learned to ride a bike, we did so by getting on the bike and trying. We each had to learn to balance. We could not learn to balance by reading a book or sitting in a class. We had to get on the bike and fall off a few times. Falling off is the problem. Our body's senses helped us to learn as we became aware of how to shift our weight to balance.

Watch a young child learn to balance on a bike without peddles. You don't teach the child the physics and biomechanics of weight and balance. You create a learning environment where they can learn from their mistakes in a safe manner. The discovery of balance may be their first independent scientific discovery. You can stand by the child, but you can't make them learn. They must do it on their own. When they do, the confidence and joy that it brings to the young child is a transformational one. I believe it is so important that to borrow from Descartes, "I balance, therefore I am."

Tacit knowledge is personal knowledge. It is how we learn to solve problems. The scientific advancement in thinking and problem solving followed Michael Polanyi's generation. Israeli psychologists Daniel Kahneman and Amos Tversky developed what they call behavioral economics. Kahneman in his book Thinking, Fast and Slow, describes what they learned. Polanyi believed that we know more than we can tell. Almost as counter-intuition, Kahneman writes, "We're blind to our blindness. We have very little idea of how little we know. We're not designed to know how little we know." Think of these two perspectives as sort of the glass half- empty / half-full. Both are trying to understand how we human beings think and in particular how to solve problems. Kahneman represents the glass-half-empty school, and Polanyi the glass half-full.

When you solve a problem, according to Kahneman, you use two different systems of thought as he describes. There is System One which "operates automatically and quickly, with little or no effort and no sense of voluntary control." I believe that this is partly what Polanyi calls tacit knowledge. System Two on the other hand is quite different. It "allocates attention to the effortful mental activities that demand it, including complex computations." The problem of problem solving is that we don't have very good tools for the kind of logical problem solving that can be taught to every person. This is why I developed the Circle of Impact to be a problem solving method that has universal application and value. Kahneman describes these two systems of thinking as intuitive and logical. We need both. System Two needs more work to benefit us.

The more we work at System Two the greater System One grows. Solving mind problems with real-world benefits expands our awareness and our tacit, intuition knowledge. I have learned that people who apply the Circle of Impact in their life and work at some point no longer have to consciously think through the process. It becomes second nature. Like riding a bike. They just see the interaction between the three dimensions of ideas, relationships, and structure.

Therefore as we begin to look more closely at problem solving, I believe we can say the following.

- The world is open to us because it always in transition.

- We learn through the experience of being people who live physically aware of the world through our senses.

- In order to learn through experience, we must learn to think logically and inquisitively.

- We must be open to what the world presents to us each day.

- As a result, we need tools for learning that strengthens how we engage the world.

Chapter Five:
Ways of Solving Problems

Why We Love Solving Problems

What is a problem? It is the missing piece of a puzzle. It is the reason our expectations are not being fulfilled. It is a question about something that doesn't make sense to us. It is the unknown path to the completion of a complex project. It is a discovery process.

We love the challenge of crossword puzzles, games of solitaire and Candy Crush on our phones, and chess in the park. In every game, we are challenged to figure out our next move. Solving the problem is not simply about finding out a bit of information that explains the problem. No. The solution to the problem leads to knowing what we must do because of the solution. What is our next move? What decision do we make? Do we go left, right, or straight ahead? Problem solving is not just discovering an answer, but testing our answer to see if it leads to the impact we desire.

Murder mysteries are a staple of people's summertime or commuting reading. Some of the longest-running television shows are ones like Law and Order, NCSI and Criminal Minds feature teams of investigators solving crimes. Inspiring stories of people overcoming incredible obstacles motivate us to believe we can too. We love to follow our favorite sports team because every game and every season is about solving the problem of how to win more games than the other teams. Every play, shot, or pitch is a problem seeking the answer of a first down, a basket, or a strikeout or home run.

Why We Avoid Solving Problems

Problem solving tests our knowledge, our situational awareness, and our ability to think logically and creatively. It involves both strategic (long term) and tactical (action-oriented) thinking. When the problem is strategic, the solution can require a significant transition in focus and allocation of resources. When the problem is tactical, the solution may require a series of incremental changes. This is the difference between big picture problems and small ones.

My experience shows me that what we don't like is having to implement the solutions to our problems. When the problem is an academic question that a philosopher might ponder and write a book on, we find that interesting. Yet, when we are, shall we say, forced to solve a problem that will require change, then we are far more hesitant. The greater the consequence the less confident we are that we can solve it. Daniel Kahneman points to this. "We have no reason to expect the quality of intuition to improve with the importance of the problem.

Perhaps the contrary: high stake problems are likely to involve powerful emotions and strong impulses to action." This explains what I see. Our resistance to change, even when we know it is needed, is not about logic, but about our emotions. When our emotions become involved, our sense of identity and well-being become involved.

As a consultant, I saw individuals and groups engage in problem solving and planning, and then do nothing. For a long time, I wondered about this. I am a pretty analytical person. The logic of our conclusions validated the accuracy of the actions to take. But they didn't take them. The reasons can be summarized by a couple of sayings that I often hear. One is "people want what people want." In other words, even when they know something is not in their best interest people will choose it because it is what they want. The other saying is "people don't change until the pain of changing is less than the pain of staying the same." Of course, this is not a matter of logic, but of perception. The unknown future will almost always look more painful than whatever our current problems suggest.

The solution to a problem is often a change that we need to make. Change is a problem for us. I have found that many people would rather suffer from a persistent problem than take on the consequences of change that the solution requires.

We fail to solve our problems because we choose to avoid change. The consequence can be far greater than the problem itself. The Senior Vice President of a client company described how this behavior had affected his work.

Two employees at his company, one a machine operator, the other a person charged with the maintenance of the machine, were in dispute about the care and use of the machine. Their supervisor avoided solving the disagreement by passing it up the chain of command. His reason was that he didn't know what to do. Eventually, after being passed from supervisor to manager, the problem ended up on the Senior Vice President's desk. The problem which began as a disagreement, a simple problem, between two people had now become an issue between the company and its union. A culture of problem avoidance had developed. A pattern of behavior by the executive team had restricted the ability of employees, supervisors, and managers from taking action to solve problems that immediately affected them.

Change avoidance doesn't just happen in isolated situations where the consequences are not clear. It can also constitute a culture that takes root in an organization. The real problem is not change avoidance, but rather our self-understanding. How we understand ourselves is the foundation of all our behaviors.

The Circle of Impact is not just another management diagram. It is a way to see how to change. As my experience taught me long ago, organizations mirror the psychology of the people who work there. Change our perspective and we can change our behavior. Change our behavior and we can change the world.

Seeking Real Solutions

I have spent my life as an observer of the behaviors of people and organizations. Not as an academic researcher, but as a guy interested in how to support these same people in their diverse life endeavors. I located this interest within the field of leadership because there is no field quite broad enough that provides a way of seeing the big picture. This is why I say that "all leadership begins with personal initiative to create impact that makes a difference that matters." Our individual lives are defined by our actions and the impact of those actions. However, we don't start with what should I do? We start with what needs to get done. Yes, it is a subtle, yet important distinction. In other words, we begin by identifying the problem to be solved. No problem? No solution.

The Circle of Impact is the result of identifying those patterns of behavior that I observed. The patterns revealed how we look at the environments in which we live and work. It reveals the reality of the situations that we are in.

There were five different ways of problem solving that I have observed people utilizing.

- Mechanistic: Break things apart and find the faulty part

- Intuitive realization

- Responsibility avoidance through scapegoating

- Affirmation through confirmation bias

- Logical (analytic / mathematical / algorithmic)

Each type of problem solving method can become the default method for us. We get used to doing things a certain way. We treat all our problems as if they are the same. We bend the problem to our will. We construct a kind of enclosed mind space. In effect, we play a game. We acknowledge what we are used to seeing and ignore the factors that are beyond our experience. It is similar to the lyric from Paul Simon's 1960s hit, The Boxer, where he writes, "People believe what they want to believe and disregard the rest." This line has stuck with me because it so often explains the pattern of behavior I see in people and their organizations.

The further we go down this path, the more detached we can become from reality. We construct our own preferred reality. Social philosophers call this a simulacrum. It is a simulated reality. So much of our lives are lived looking at a screen, much of what we see there is a simulation of reality. Video games simulate violence. Pornography simulates sexual interplay. Politics as presented through the screen simulates a perception about society intended to influence voters. Televised sports are less about the game and more about the simulated reality of the world that surrounds the game. Is any of it real? Yes, to a certain degree. If the simulacrum of a life lived through the screen was not a representation of reality, we would not believe it. The difference is that simulated reality is never representative of the whole reality of a situation.

We cannot see what others can see. We can only see our preferred reality. The longer we do so, the more sophisticated this simulated world becomes. The problem with a simulated reality is that it does not ultimately resolve the questions that we have.

French theorist Guy Debord sees these simulations that he calls a spectacle as an "affirmation of appearance." Problem solving becomes a show of solving problems. The simulacra of problem solving is more important than the solution.

How did I come to see this gap between reality and a simulated one? It started as I found people unwilling to address real problems that confronted them. In one of my early jobs, I had a supervisor who would create problems with my performance that were fabrications. For months, I laid awake the night before my supervisory meeting wondering how I would be attacked. The realization came to me that none of this was about my performance, but rather a projection of his authority over me. It was a simulation of control that did not affect the work that I actually did. When I finally understood what was really going on, I called him on it.

In other work environments, I'd see how people clearly lied to themselves about a past decision that created their current problems. They could not look with self-criticism at their situation. They could not see the patterns of behavior that created a range of problems going back decades that created the problematic conditions that we were currently facing. Their perception was a simulated reality that ultimately led to the reality of having to close their business.

My point is that a simulated environment of problem solving has a negative effect on us. It encourages a pattern of avoidance, even delusion, about the real issues that we face. It creates unhealthy detachment from what is real. We can talk ourselves into believing that we are solving a problem, when we are creating a larger one than before. As a result, reality can be a harsh teacher.

Daniel Kahneman's System 1 thinking process and Michael Polanyi's tacit knowledge operate at the intuitive level. This intuitive knowledge can also trick us into believing that we see things clearly. If we live only by intuition, we will find ourselves living in a simulated reality to avoid the realities that are present. We must learn from experience. We need to ask questions. We need to be skeptical of our motivations for taking particular actions. We need to test the assumptions that we have derived from people of expert opinion. The benefit is that we get much better feedback by embracing reality than living in the attractive fictional world of a simulated reality.

As I addressed these situations with clients, it became important to develop a method for revealing reality into stories we tell ourselves. I call this method Impact Day. It is disciplined problem solving method that reveals what we believe intuitively about our circumstances. The process trains the participant to ask questions that help us to discover the reality of any situation. To ask questions is to critique our own assumptions. When we ask questions in relationship with others, where we share a common purpose and vision, then we have the opportunity to see things that others cannot see.

Five Methods for Solving Problems

There are five problem solving types that I have identified. The problems can be simple or complex. However, we must be able to look at situations and see them for what they really are. We need to acquire the ability to see how these dimensions interact with one another.

Together, we gather information, reflect upon it, and identify a solution that we can act upon. The Circle of Impact is one tool and the Impact Day process another for seeing these dimensions interact with one another. Being able to take a problem and create clarity brings motivation for impact.

Let us look at each method to understand how they solve problems.

Mechanistic: Break things apart and find the faulty part

This is a type of analytic method that takes apart the problem to find the faulty part. There is no holistic perspective that guides the process. This method is derived from the scientific method. However, its application is not always appropriate to the situation.

In my short book, All Crises Are Local: Understanding the COVID-19 Global Pandemic, I look at the response by public health and governmental authorities from a systems point of view. My criticism is that their problem solving method broke apart society into discrete separate parts, like public health, economics, education, and public safety. The reality is that societies don't operate as a collection of interchangeable parts but as a body, as something whole and undivided. The viral pandemic response ignored this reality in favor of the simulacrum of public health. This simulated response caused the "cure" to be worse than the disease. Even as vaccines have become available, the problem that caused the pandemic has not been solved.

Unless we are solving a problem that is mechanistic in nature, like an engine failure, or a process of delivering paychecks to employees on time, most of the situations that we face are not mechanistic, but synthetic. All aspects of a group or a situation are intertwined like a piece of fabric. Other ways of problem solving may be better suited to finding solutions depending upon the problem. It is often this approach that becomes the default one because it does not require the capacity to address the complexity inherent in many problems.

Intuitive realization

We often make decisions based upon our "gut" response. We feel something is not quite right, and so we decide not to take the job. We react automatically as a learned response.

If during childhood, we were often shamed for making minor mistakes, we learn to cope by seeing which response gets our preferred reaction. We may verbally strike back or detach ourselves emotionally to think more analytically. We learn from experience. Though experience is not always the best teacher. Regardless, we intuitively learn to respond in particular ways by learning what works and what doesn't.

This is somewhat like the intuitive responses that Daniel Kahneman and Michael Polanyi describe. We are offered a new position at the company. We decide not to accept the offer, even though by every indication it is an advancement. We know that something is missing even though we cannot say what it is. Yet, we can feel it. We just can't put our finger on it.

It is that same feeling that we have sitting in a team meeting realizing that I am missing some essential information that everyone else seems to know. Our intuition asks, "Am I the only one in the dark about this?" If the team has established trust, then you ask them, "I missing something here?" Then, we find out that this is new information for the team. We are relieved. However, if the team is built around internal competition, then our focus will shift from the missing information to who is manipulating the team by withholding pertinent information. In the moment, all we may have available to us is the intuitive judgment which may be based upon incomplete information and a prejudicial perspective.

The key for intuition to serve us well as a problem solving method centers on our self- awareness. The lack of self-understanding is a key reason teams and leaders fail in their problem solving responsibilities. I have worked with leaders who hide behind a sophisticated personal brand story. They are a representation of a simulated character. There is a barrier of appearance that stands between them and others. As a result, it is impossible for the real problem to be resolved. Instead, a solution is established that supports the leader's brand. The result is a loss of trust and a sense of disequilibrium by the team. In other words, we trust our intuition to tell us who we can trust and who we cannot.

Regardless of what our "gut" tells us, we need to discern what the real situation is by utilizing other problem solving methodologies.

Responsibility avoidance through scapegoating

This problem solving methodology is an avoidance model. The idea is that whatever problems exist are secondary to the importance of maintaining power and control. The French/American historian Rene' Girard, the foremost writer on scapegoating, locates this behavior in the human desire to imitate others. We learn by following or imitating others. Lacking self-awareness we follow the person who seems most attractive or influential. It is the secret behind mass movements. The followers desire to be like the person in power. They become subservient as they strive to be like him or her. Girard calls this mimetic desire. The closer we get to be like the one we seek to imitate, the greater the conflict, for our goals are a replication of their goals.

In the function of a business or a corporate team, the preservation of power and institutional standing can substitute for shared processes of problem solving. Countless times during a consulting project, the senior leader would display a kind of supportive indifference towards our work. When I asked what their desired impact is, I would never get a straight answer. The goal was not essentially about the difference the group could make. Rather, it was about making sure the internal operations of the organization served the interests of the leader.

When a staff person or a board member would get too close to identifying this situation as a critical problem, that person would be terminated or isolated within the group. As a result, scapegoating became a problem solving methodology.

Scapegoating functions as a pattern of behavior. When competition grows between members of a team, a family, or in any institutional setting, a dynamic of change occurs. At first, it could be healthy as differing perspectives open up possibilities for solutions to problems. However, if the competition persists, then violence of a social and institutional kind results. The purpose of scapegoating is to return the institution to a peaceful, unified state. Of course, peace and unity are terms open to interpretation based upon the values of the people involved.

When scapegoating takes hold in an organization, control becomes the problem that must be resolved. It is why corruption grows. Authority can become authoritarian. Accountability is easily lost. Girard wrote that "When scandals proliferate, human beings become so obsessed with their rivals that they lose sight of the objects for which they compete and begin to focus angrily on one another." He points to the hiddenness of this behavior. "Having a scapegoat means not knowing that we have one." We scapegoat when we demonize or cancel people for their views and different perspectives. It is a type of solution that resolves internal problems of power and control by removing those who are a threat to those who are in power.

Affirmation through Confirmation Bias

Confirmation bias, as defined by Wikipedia, "is the tendency to search for, interpret, favor, and recall information in a way that confirms or supports one's prior beliefs or values. People tend to unconsciously select information that supports their views, but ignore non-supportive or contradicting information." During my time as an organizational consultant, I would enter into an organizational environment as an outsider. My job was to identify problem areas and opportunities for change that would benefit the organization. I came to realize that many of these projects were what we might call "window-dressing" or "gaslighting." The project presented the image of the organization and its leaders as forward-thinking, progressive change agents. In reality, they were looking for reasons not to change. This is what confirmation bias looks like.

Confirmation bias is really a bias against change. The result is that problems get ignored. Opportunities are missed. Having observed so many leaders and organizations fall prey to their confirmation bias, I came to realize that change was not the problem. It is rather a lack of clarity about why the business exists and what its impact should be. In other words, we need to embrace change.

What does this look like? It begins by recognizing that we are all in transition. All of us. All the time. Opportunities for growth are not found by doing the same thing over and over again expecting different results. This is how physicist Albert Einstein defined insanity. Rather we should change when it is clear that we should. This strikes at the heart of confirmation bias. I am saying that confirmation bias only serves to hold us back.

Some of those who have written about confirmation bias place a problematic emphasis on beliefs and values. If we are in constant need of outside confirmation that our values matter, then our values are not clearly understood or applied. A true values perspective defines a person or group's purpose for impact. It provides the foundation for how the members of the organization are going to work with one another. Only when we are clear and convinced that what we believe is sound, will we find ourselves in a position of openness to change.

Logical (analytic / mathematical / algorithmic)

In some respects, we come full circle with this approach to problem solving. Where the mechanistic is also logical as it breaks the problem down into parts, a traditional analytical approach looks to logic to determine whether the solution to a problem makes sense.

It is this approach that I find practiced more often in a business context. It can produce clarity of perspective, understanding of the consequences of a decision, and provide the insight needed to design a plan of action. This is what we need in problem solving.

Yet, the problem with logic is that it can only be the way I just describe when the people involved are clear about their purpose and the goals of the organization. Logic is not a check on bad problem solving or worse corruption. I see logic as always "internally correct." By this I mean, logic leads to the conclusion that the data provides us. What we exclude from our problem solving processes matters.

The Circle of Impact is based upon the inter-working of the three dimensions of ideas, relationships, and structure. When I speak of structure I am speaking of two types. There is the organization's structure and the social or cultural structure of the organization.

The pattern of behavior that I observed from the earliest point of my career is the tendency to primarily focus on organizational structure in planning and problem solving. In larger organizations, this meant a dependence on numbers as a measure of the state of the organization. It was clear to me that numbers don't tell the whole story. They tell a logical story to a point. However, there is always missing data.

I am making a distinction here between quantitative data and qualitative data. One way to distinguish these two types of information is to say the former tells us what and the latter why.

Recall how I'd asked leaders what their impact was? Impact is a qualitative perspective focused on changes that are made that matter. It is why ideas and relationships matter. They are not subservient to numbers. They explain what the numbers cannot.

Logic is a key tool in problem solving. However, it must include a willingness to be skeptical about our assumptions and conclusions. This is why it is important to have a standard for judgment that can be applied to every facet of the organization. Impact is that standard. With every problem, we should ask, "What do we want to change?" Proper logic will lead us to see when our solution shows us that it is a change that does not align well with our purpose for impact.

Learning through Experience

How do we come to learn to solve our problems? As I have looked back upon my life, I don't believe I ever had anyone teach me to do so. We learn by trial and error, by experience. As the world has become more open, information more available, interaction across cultures a daily experience, we need a way that can provide clarity from the broadest possible context. More than ever, we need to see a big picture of the world in which we live and solve problems.

Each of these five methods of problem solving methods emerged through experience. The Circle of Impact is no different. In the next section, I show how to solve problems using the Impact Day problem solving method. I use the name Impact Day because the aim, whether it is in problem solving, planning, or training leaders, is to create impact today, right now.

Chapter Six:
Impact Day: A Fresh
Approach to Problem
Solving

How I Discovered Problem Solving

As a child, not only did I assemble models of cars, air-planes, and ships, I read a lot of biographies. Two that I reread often were on Madame Marie Curie, a pioneer-ing scientist in the field of radioactivity, and Wilbur and Orville Wright, pioneers in early aviation and the first to fly a motorized airplane. Their stories of innovation in new fields of endeavor inspired in me a love for the adventure of discovery. Like the Star Trek motto, "to go where no man or woman has gone before."

It was also the time when the adventure of space had captured the country's attention. As a nine-year-old, I remember hearing a portion of President John F. Kennedy's Go-To-The-Moon speech on the news. He said,

> "But why, some say, the moon? Why choose this as our goal? And they may well ask why climb the highest mountain? Why, 35 years ago, fly the Atlantic? … We choose to go to the moon. We choose to go to the moon in this decade and do the other things, not because they are easy, but because they are hard, because that goal will serve to organize and measure the best of our energies and skills …"

Being a problem solver elevates us to become the best we can be. I know that is a tired ole cliché. For many people who speak of such things, they don't do the hard work to go where no one has gone before. I saw this early in my life. People who talk a great game, but rarely deliver when the game is on the line.

Problem solving is more than the techniques. It can be something that defines us as persons. Think back over the course of your life. What challenges did you face to required you to test, to organize, and to measure the best of your energies and skills? This is the spirit of impact that I began to see as the answer to the problems that I found in organizations.

It was a natural thing for me to go start my own consulting practice. Even though I had never run a business nor been a consultant. My reasons had to do with the problems that I saw originating in traditional assumptions about leadership and the management of organizations. Those assumptions are still prevalent today and are the source of the problems that I still see plaguing people, organizations, and communities.

Why do these problems persist? Why do people once they identify a solution back away from implementing it? What ways of thinking inhibit problem solving processes? Why do incremental changes seem to be emotionally satisfying, yet not really address the deeper structural issues of problems? What effect do executive attitudes have on employee willingness to solve problems?

A Universal Problem Solving Tool

Out of the experience of asking questions like these, the Circle of Impact model of leadership was born. The model represents a picture of three dimensions that command our attention in every arena of our lives. They are the dimensions of ideas, relationships, and organizational structure. Whenever you have a problem, its origin is in one or more of these dimensions.

The three dimensions are a way of seeing the whole of life. Every aspect is incorporated into one of these dimensions. The distinctiveness of the three can be understood simply. We all think, imagine, or conceptualize what life is. We develop relationships where we communicate, collaborate, and congregate as families, communities, networks, and societies. We organize the world around the structures of organizations. Every problem or opportunity is represented by one or more of these dimensions.

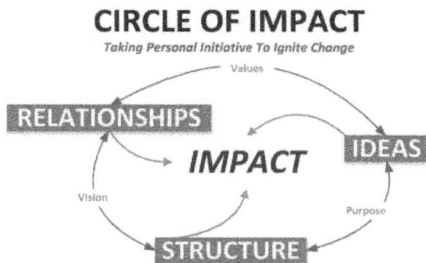

CIRCLE OF IMPACT
Taking Personal Initiative To Ignite Change

The Circle of Impact is designed as a simple tool for planning, problem solving and training for people to be impact leaders. The focus is on identifying the impact we desire. Impact is a change that makes a difference.

The model is interested in identifying how each of the dimensions contributes to this impact. The goal is to align the three dimensions for impact.

The Impact Day methodology applies the Circle of Impact model as a universal problem solving tool. However, to really make this work for you, it requires a willingness to take responsibility for the problems that you want to solve. This is why "all leadership begins with personal initiative." In this sense, the first problem to solve is our own motivation and willingness to do the hard work of change.

My experience convinces me that anyone can learn to solve problems without reservation or fear. If you could learn to do so your life will gain a degree of purpose that builds confidence that we can face any obstacle. Wherever you face fear, you have a problem that the Circle of Impact can resolve.

Problem solving is a strategy for living in a world that is in constant transition. It should not be the last thing you turn to when you have no other options. It should be how you approach your life and work.

Consider what it would be like if everyone on your team or company could be problem solvers. Imagine what it would be like if everyone in your family learned to solve problems. Can you see how it could change the nightly dinner table conversation? If we learned to be better problem solvers, I believe we would less likely to blame others, looking for scapegoats, and see problems coming before they reach a critical stage.

More specifically, we'll discover that situations that we once saw as problems have become opportunities. Opportunities to fulfill our purpose and realize the desires that we have for a life of meaning and impact. We move from being stuck in place to constantly moving forward.

This method digs deep into the reasons for the problems. Yet, does not get lost in being overly abstract or as I often hear, "getting lost in the weeds." The focus throughout is to understand the problem from the perspective of the impact that the solution can create.

If a problem solving methodology is not practical, it isn't solving problems. It is just kicking the can down the street for someone else to pick up and try to fix it. As a result, the best way to approach learning a problem solving methodology is to solve a problem.

The Impact Day Process

Impact Day has three basic steps.

First, we identify the problem. Second, we decide what kind of problem it is. And, third, we ask direct questions related to change and impact. We end up by reframing the original problem and drafting a strategy to resolve it.

We begin by asking what the problem is. It seems that this should be simple. It is not easy to clarify what our problem actually is. One of the goals of the Impact Day process is to clarify what the exact problem is.

Often I find that the first attempt to describe a problem has more to do with the symptoms of them. The point is to establish a starting point. By the end of the process, we will see the problem differently. The whole idea is to make clear what is going on so that we can make the right decisions about what to do.

Here's an example that I frequently use. It is a problem that we all have. In various ways, this problem manifests itself as a perfect example to see how the Impact Day process works.

> *Problem: There is a breakdown in com-munication within the team that is affect-ing client relationships.*

Once we have decided what our problem is, we ask, "What kind of problem is this?" Is this an Idea problem, a Relationship problem, or a Structure problem?

Our initial intuition may lead us to think that this is a relationship problem. However, our intuition may not always be right. We need to dig deeper into what is happening with the three dimensions to understand where the problem originates.

Measuring Impact of the Three Dimensions

We measure each of the dimensions through the lens of quality. Why is quality important? Is quality too subjective an idea? Do not quantitative measures provide a clearer perspective? Quantitative questions measure how resources are being utilized and developed. People, in general, measure their lives quantitatively? What numbers do they track? In particular, they measure their finances, making sure they pay their bills, file their taxes, and save and invest for retirement. They want to be able to have money to buy a car, go on vacation, and send their children to college. However, is that the measure of a life?

People are conscious of quality of life issues. Quality is a measure of the strength to create change that makes a difference that matters. Numbers follow quality. People save in order to buy the things that manifest a quality life. A place at the beach. Season tickets to the local pro sports team. Winter vacations in Mexico. Quality of life could be described in terms of philanthropy and charitable giving. Establishing a financial trust to provide for grandkids after our passing. Quality of life is defined by the values that matter to us. Quality measures track whether what we do, how we do it, and with whom we do it, fulfill goals that define who we are.

Let's go a step deeper. How do we measure our life purpose quantitatively? It certainly isn't by collecting multiple purposes. No. It is the opposite. We want our purpose to be clear and focused. We create clarity by identifying how our purpose points us toward the impact we want to achieve.

How do you measure your life? Is it by how much money you earn? Is it by how long a life you hope to live? Is it how many things you own, or how many people you are connected to on social media? Those quantitative measures don't capture the quality of our relationships, nor the quality of the life we live each day. Instead, they tell us whether the structure of our life can produce the quality of life that we desire.

We should then be asking: What is my purpose for impact?

Impact is the measure of the quality of the structure of our lives. In a business, we can measure structure quantitatively by sales numbers, profit and loss results, and industry standing. Those numbers don't account for impact. How do we understand 5% growth of revenue during a calendar year from the perspective of impact?

How does the structure of our work impact our relationships? What is the impact you want for your clients? How about the impact your work has on your family? These are quality measures that are important for understanding the context of the problems we face. Every problem functions within the context of some structure.

We can look at structure from two perspectives. Think of them as external and internal structures. The external is the organizational superstructure. The internal is the social life that fills the structure. It is the culture that the ideas and relationship dimensions create to give the external structure its life.

There are four functions to every organizational structure. There are product sales and services, operations to support that function, finances that fund those functions, and governance to guide all of them. Each needs quantitative measures. However, to really understand how the organization is functioning, we need quality measures. What is the impact of our products, our services, our finances, and our governance function? What changes do those functions have that make a difference that matters? Clarify the change you want, and the problem areas will reveal themselves.

The social structure forms the culture of a company and of a family. Think of this culture as how people relate to one another and to the organizations. If the culture is problem-filled, we can see it in a lack of respect, trust, and mutual accountability between people. Where the quality is present we will find "a persistent, residual culture of values." Values are the glue to culture and guide what our purpose and vision for impact should be. As a result, the social structure will be a culture of clear values that will persist because those values reside in the relationships of the people.

Three Dimensions	Ideas	Relationships	Structure
	↓	↓	↓
Quality Measures	Clarity	Respect, Trust, and Mutual Accountability	Impact
	↓	↓	↓
What is Missing?	Understanding about Values, Purpose, Impact, and Vision	Quality Teamwork	Change that makes a difference that matters.

By asking what kind of problem ours is, we look for the quality present in the three dimensions. This chart provides a way to analyze our situation to see where a problem may exist.

The first step in problem solving is to understand what the problem is and its source. For the process, it is sufficient to write a single sentence stating our perception at this point as to what the problem is. Our understanding doesn't have to be complete or perfect. This statement is just a starting point.

Chapter Seven:
The Five Questions
Everyone Must Ask

The third step of the Impact Day process is focuses on questions that we ask to unlock the insights of the Circle of Impact model can provide us. The questions we ask must open up our perception to see the problem from a broader perspective. The Five Questions That Everyone Must Ask were developed for this purpose.

The Five Questions are:

> 1. What has Changed? How am I/We in Transition?
> 2. What is My/Our Impact?
> 3. Who have I/We Impacted?
> 4. What Opportunities do I/We have?
> 5. What Obstacles do I/We face? What Problems have I/We created?

These questions are designed to be asked about everything we do. They can be used for problem solving, planning, and to frame strategic conversations.

Let's look at this in the context of our problem what has to do with team communication. You are the team leader. You know there is a problem. You don't know why or how it developed. You have a team meeting scheduled for later this week.

Your first step in preparing for the meeting is to ask the Five Questions.

- What has changed with our team? How are we in transition? Can we identify a date or an event where things changed?

- What is the impact of this change? What difference, positively or negatively is this change?

- Who is being impacted by this problem? Team members? Customers? Others?

- If we were to resolve this problem, what opportunities would we have?

- What problems have we created based on the quality measures of the Circle of Impact? What obstacles do we face to resolving this issue?

This meeting represents one step along the path of transition that has already begun. You take your team through the same Five Question process. Following the meeting, you evaluate the process by asking the Five Questions again. Let's dig deeper into how to understand each question.

Question One:
What has Changed?
How am I/We in Transition?

One of the five principles of the Circle of Impact is that we are in transition, all of us, all the time. Transition is different than change. We transition along a path of changes. It is a constant fluctuation in the situations we find ourselves in. Change is the points of transition along the way.

We ask "What has changed?" and "How are we in transition?" We want to look back in time to a point where we first identified that there was a problem. We want to look at this timeframe as one of change from initial awareness to our decision to address the problem. It may be a few hours, several months, or many years. The longer the time we set, the more time we need to spend identifying the moments of transition that led to the present moment.

In our example, communication began to erode after the members of the team changed eighteen months ago. The pace of work and the stress of implementing a new program did not allow for time for the team to form as a team. The result was increasing difficulty in communication. Seeing when the team's communication began to decline does not identify the problem. It only identifies a time frame in which it did. This is why it is important to ask all five questions before making a judgment as to the problem.

This question is showing the team in transition in multiple ways. It is important to write down your observations. We've identified two. The change in the makeup of the team and the decline in communication. Are there other ways the team has been in transition? Yes. There is also the new initiative that was given to the team at the same time the membership in the team changed. There may be other ways we can see the team in transition.

If we are unsatisfied with the changes and transition that we have identified, then we can ask the question about each of the three dimensions.

- What has changed about our perception (Ideas) about this problem? Are we clearer or more confused?

- What has changed in our Relationships? How are our Relationships as a team in transition? Are respect, trust, and mutual accountability growing or declining?

- What has changed within the Structure of our team or company? How is our team or company in transition? Are we clear about what the impact of the new initiative is to create?

Asking these questions reveals what may be hidden. We need to see below the surface. This first question begins the process of revealing what may have been hidden by the day-to-day pace of work.

Projecting forward this question can be restated for planning purposes. We can ask: What Change do we want to see in the future? How do we want to Transition from where we are to where need to be? If we ask this question as a team at each point of the process, we have begun to improve communication by helping everyone to be on the same page.

Question Two:
What is My/Our Impact?

If we are doing a simple review of the past, we want to know the impact of our work or our team or some other aspect of who we are. However, if we are seeking to solve a problem, we want to understand how the problem has impacted us. What changes took place that caused us to see the situation as a problem.

In other words, we are taking the question, "What is my impact?", and applying it to a particular context. We can ask this question in the context of a problem. Or it could be in the context of an annual review of our employees. Or it could be asked in the context of the future. The context of our questions matter.

If we are not clear about how to ask this question, like in the first question, we turn to asking the question of the three dimensions.

What is the impact of my ideas, my relationships, or the structure of our work? If that still does not lead us to find clarity of perspective then we take a step to a deeper level. We ask the question in the following manner.

- How have our values impacted this problem? Are we clear about our team's values?

- What does our team's purpose for impact reveal about this problem? Do we have a clearly identified purpose for impact?

- How is this problem a product of the presence or absence of respect, trust, and mutual accountability within our team and with our customers?

- Is this problem a result of a breakdown in some aspect of our team's structure?

I could continue to create questions that we could be asking. We are like those detectives on television who know just the right questions to ask to get to the bottom of "who-done-it?"

It is true that many people will find asking so many questions a waste of time. We, then, ask the question, "What is the impact of their resistance to asking questions?" My experience points to an attitude that this is not my responsibility. If this is their perspective, then this is an aspect of the problem pointing toward a part of the solution.

When a team member or employee does not see problem solving as an essential part of their job, then the impact of their work will be less than it should. It points to a lack of awareness. It doesn't mean that they don't see the problem. Rather, they don't see how they can address it from their role within the company.

The question we should ask at this point is not why are they resistant to taking responsibility for problem solving, but rather how do the three dimensions contribute to a culture where problem solving is someone else's problem? This line of questioning resembles the mechanistic breaking apart of situations. However, what we are looking for is not the faulty part, but rather the point of origin of the problem causing a particular type of impact throughout.

I hope you see that this question is vital to understanding the transition of change that has led to the emergence of the problem in question.

Question Three:
Who have I/We Impacted?

Problems don't happen in a vacuum. They happen in the context of our relationship with people. This question was created because I found in my client's work that people were quite often unaware of the extent of the impact that their decisions had upon people. As I would try to track down what their initial perception was, I discovered that their perception was limited to themselves and a vague sense of what were called stakeholders.

Ask the question, "Who is impacted by this problem?" - Take a blank piece of paper and map out all those who are. There are three levels to consider. One concerns those directly impacted who are also responsible. Two identifies those who are secondarily impacted by some delay or a greater sense of isolation from the group. Three represents the organizations that are impacted.

By identifying these people, we are possibly creating a team of people who could gather together as problem solvers. Ensuring that the full range of constituents are represented creates an environment of shared responsibility. This means that the dimension of relationships has become a resource in creating the solution to our problem. In creating this team, we want to ensure that it is based upon respect, trust, and mutual accountability. How do we do this?

We must be clear about why solving this problem is important. Our Why in this regard is defined by the values that lead us to identify this situation as a problem.

The Purpose of the Five Questions

The Five Questions as a problem solving tool can be divided into two parts. The first three questions help us clarify the question. The last two questions help us identify the path to the solution.

We ask the Five Questions not just to clarify what the problem is. We also want to establish an alignment of the three dimensions of the Circle of Impact. My experience shows me that every problem involves all three dimensions. To solve our problems, we need to see how the dimensions contribute to both the problem and the solution.

Developing the Circle of Impact in the context of working with clients and my own life, I discovered that a solution to a problem is rarely in the problem itself. Let say that again. It is important. The solution to a problem is not in the dimension that we identify as the source of the problem

If our team communication problem is a relationship problem, we can't just go and try to fix the relationships. Instead, we turn to the ideas and structure dimensions to discover possible solutions. What does this look like?

Our team communication problem will manifest itself in the quality of relationships. We will see disrespect, mistrust, and the refusal to be accountable to the team as a pattern of behavior. If we see those behaviors, then we know we have a relationship problem. You cannot enforce those qualities as a solution. You must build them into relationships. How do we do this?

We first turn to the Ideas dimension. We begin by establishing a core ideology of values. This step should have been done when the team was formed. Instead, what I see is that teams form around the structure of their work. As a result, there is no recognition about what values will define us as a team. Not only that, the purpose is not for impact, but rather for the quantitative measures of the organization's structure. In effect, we are defined by the institution, not by our values or our relationships with one another.

The quality measures of respect, trust, and mutual accountability are the products of shared values. This means that one of the requirements for membership on the team is commitment to the core values of the team. The implication is that dissension from the core values will cause division and conflict between members of the team. In some organizations, violation of the core values can be cause for dismissal from the team or termination from the organization. It sounds harsh. Yet, the damage is done when values conflict is the impact that we would be able to identify from the first three questions.

We creating a solution to a relationship problem within a team by first establishing a core set of values whose impact can be measured as respect, trust, and mutual accountability.

This is only part of the solution. The team also needs a structure where those values can create an environment where respect, trust, and mutual accountability are promoted and valued. We are looking at both the social structure and the team structure for this part of the solution.

The social structure of the team is a culture derived from the shared values. It results in "a persistent, residual culture of values." These shared values persist because they reside in the relationships of the team. Every team will be different, but the experience of respect and trust are the real quality measures.

Note how in the formation of the team I have said nothing about the business impact of the team. Yet, every team has a business structure. Its members are chosen to fulfill specific roles. However, the team needs to have a shared sense of purpose for the goals to be met. It is for this reason that the team needs to be able to define for themselves what their impact should be. To do this the Five Questions can be a tool that they use to establish and manage their relationships as a team.

Question Four:
What Opportunities do I/We have?

With this question, we are not thinking about just any opportunity, but opportunity for impact. The longer version of this question is "What opportunities do we have right now because of the impact that we have already create?" Apply it to every person in your organization. What opportunities for impact do they individually have? To understand this question, we need to understand impact creation within the context of the Circle of Impact model of leadership.

Leadership from this perspective is not a role or a title, but how we function in our lives and work. To make sense of this transition, we need a new definition of leadership. From the perspective of the Circle of Impact model, all leadership begins with personal initiative to create impact that makes a difference that matters.

Opportunities for impact are not singular, but multiple and grown out of our purpose for impact. It is not just any impact, but the change that makes a difference that matters that conforms to our values and stated purpose.

The values component of a business is foundational to this question. As we become clear about our values, we become clear about the impact of the organization defined as our purpose.

Those values are shared values by the team who focus their individual initiatives toward a shared purpose for impact. Each person is focused on their impact creation from within the role that they perform for the business. Senior executive roles, as a result, shift from actions of delegation and direction down through the organization to the facilitation and creation of a culture leadership up through the organization's structure. The impact of these complementary changes is the expansion of opportunities while at the same time focusing on the company's impact.

As we look at our example of a team's communication problem, what opportunities do we have there? Recall that we have identified relationships as the focal point of our problem. Respect, trust, and mutual accountability are missing. We have already discussed clarifying our values and purpose. Of course, people can give "lip-service" to these ideas. You can't force people to adopt certain values. You must use persuasion to change their perspective. You can manage according to the values of the company. When company values are understood through the lens of behaviors then termination for failure to uphold the values can be enforced. This is not what we want in creating a team. The second part of our solution is structural

If a team applied these five questions to the establishment of expectations for each meeting or for the review and analysis of each person's work, a shift in perspective would take place. If managers were to supervise for impact, then we would see changes that make a difference that matters. Structure is a form of discipline to create order. The discipline of asking questions focuses on interaction. If honesty and transparency are missing in team interaction, these questions will expose it. The discipline of asking questions focused on impact makes it more difficult for team communication to be nothing more than the sharing of opinions. The asking of the Five Questions allows for mutual accountability to develop and with it respect and trust.

The answer to this question will show us our first steps toward solving the problem that we have identified. We'll know better where to invest time and resources for a solution. And we'll know when it is time to let the problem go, walking away to focus on other situations before us.

Question Five:
What Obstacles do I/We face?
What Problems have I/We created?

I was once asked why this question came last. Simple reason. No one is willing to address the problems and obstacles of their life or business until they are absolutely clear that the ultimate goal is worth the effort. If we are not clear about what we seek, our purpose for impact, then we won't take on the hard work of change. In other words, until the pain of changing is less than the pain of staying the same, we won't.

My experience with organizations is that very few people ever acknowledge their responsibility for the creation of the problem. The fragile state of the culture in many organizations is such that people don't want to be singled out for punishment or to be scapegoated.

If we don't honestly face our problems, we'll never resolve the problems that keep us from the potential impact we can create. We only grow by admitting our problems and solving them. It seems to me that the source of many of our problems are organizational structures where fear of social or organizational retribution motivates people to do just enough to remain hidden from scrutiny.

When we ask the questions "What obstacles do we face?" and "What problems have we created?", we are doing something heroic in my estimation. We making ourselves vulnerable to criticism. However, if we never do so, we never overcome the obstacles of disrespect and mistrust, of the effects of political power moves, and the constant doubt about the future of my job.

The purpose of asking these questions is to point toward the first steps that we can take to resolve the larger problem. We recognize that impact is a solution to a problem. If we begin by acknowledging our problems, resolving them, and in turn creating impact, then we are in transition in a positive way.

The Discipline of the Five Questions

I have already said that you can ask these questions in any situation. Let me reframe what I said from a suggestion into an imperative.

I am convinced that if you were to ask these questions at least once a week for the next year, your life would change. You would gain awareness, find focus, learn to be more discerning, and be able to turn away from opportunities that hold no real impact for you. In effect, life would become fuller and simpler.

An example of how this can work. A decade and a half ago my phone rang. It was my friend and leadership colleague Galba Bright, an emotional intelligence coach and consultant serving government and business in the island nations of the Caribbean. He called to tell me how the Five Questions had impacted his work. Over his computer monitor, he posted a diagram of the Five Questions that I had distributed. Galba told me that every Sunday night he would plan his week by asking the Five Questions. Over the next year, his emotional intelligence website grew to be the most visited EQ site in the world. He attributed it to asking the Five Questions. I was honored and pleased to hear his story.

Galba, who sadly is no longer with us, asked these questions once a week. It isn't his timing that matters. It is yours. Ask when you need them. However, the more you ask them, the easier the answers will come. You are training your mind to be aware of not just circumstances at this moment, but to be able to see the progression of changes over time. This is what I call transition. If you can identify the transition that you have gone through from the past to the present, you can imagine a similar transition from the present into the future. Take action on what you see.

Aligning for Impact

The curious thing about problem solving is that we think the solution is found in the problem. In our example of the team communication problem, we identified a breakdown in the team's relationship with one another. I pointed to the insight that directly addressing the relationship problem will not fix the problem. We can't force people to change. We can only provide the right kind of motivation to do so.

The Circle of Impact emerged in my mind through my consulting work. It is a picture of patterns of behavior that were inhibiting an organization's functioning. By pattern, these were behaviors that I saw in many diverse organizations. The essential pattern is a broken connection between ideas, relationships, and structure. I discovered that leaders and their organizations lack much more self-awareness than you could imagine.

Even though we spend a third to a half of every day immersed in the structure of our business, we are blind to much of it. Structure to people is like water to fish. We can't see it until its toxicity reaches a critical level. One of the behaviors related to structure is that it dominates everything. Both ideas and relationships are subordinate to structure. This is especially true in large organizations. There you can find layers and silos that block open communication vertically between the executive, the managerial, and workers and horizontally between the departments. Team communication in most organizations is a function of structure. Where it

isn't you have someone who has elevated aspects of the relational and conceptual to change how their teams function. If you want a team that exhibits respect, trust, and mutual accountability, then you have to change the structure. In order to do that, you have to be clear about why it is important. Though it is a circle of three dimensions, the beginning point for fixing structural issues is through clarification of values, purpose, and impact.

This means that every problem, every one that you or I can describe, literally everyone that we have had and will ever have, operates through the interaction of these three dimensions.

Whichever dimension we root the problem in, the other two are our resources for change. This makes problem solving simpler. Identify the problem dimension. Figure out how the other two dimensions can influence change. I realize this sounds like an over-sell. It isn't.

During a book signing, a man came to my table and challenged me to solve his problem. His work situation was changing and he didn't understand what was happening. I asked three questions, each one related to the quality measures of the three dimensions. I asked if he was clear about what his job was and why he was doing it. He said that he was clear. He was a software systems implementer for a company with a lot of government contracts. They would send him into the field to install the system. He told me that for the past couple of years, they had repeatedly been pulling him off his current project and sending him to another one. He was never completing the projects.

I asked him whether he felt the company respected his work. He said no. My last question was whether he felt the company was in trouble. I wanted to know if it was clear what their desired impact was. He said no again.

Here is a man working in an organization where all three of the dimensions are broken. It is a perfect storm of crisis and chaos. I said to him that I believed that he was being set up as the scapegoat for the company's failure. All this movement of him to different projects that he was never finishing showed that his hands were all over the failures of the company. My advice to him was to leave and find another job. He told me that he realized that this is what was happening. He had already left the company for a new job.

The solution to every problem begins with clarity. We need to be absolutely clear about why we are in the situation we are in. We need to be self-aware about our own contribution to the problem. We need to understand our relationship to other people's problems. For even if the problem is not directly related to us, we are impacted by it.

This problem solving methodology fits into a program called Impact Day. It also includes planning and self-awareness for leadership impact. Once you learn or become practiced in the method, there is never any reason to be in the dark or out-of-the-loop. You actually may intentionally be excluded from understanding what is going on. However, by being aware that you are, you can establish an understanding that prepares you to respond effectively when called upon.

Chapter Eight:
Problem Solvers are
Persons of Impact

The Ultimate Solution is Impact

Everybody solves problems. We do this in order to make it through a day. We solve the problem of what to wear, what to eat, what route to take to work, what order of tasks to do today, and on. The answer to every decision is a solution to a problem. We all solve problems. And we can certainly learn how to solve them better.

However, not all of us are problem solvers. We are not self-consciously planning our day to solve problems that resolve larger questions. When the scientists who gathered for the Solvay Conference in 1927, they collaborated on questions of physics. Big problems that are beyond most of us to understand, much less solve.

We don't have to be Nobel Prize winning physicists in order to be considered a problem solver. Instead, we can look at the world beyond our fingertips, that world that may not have a direct connection to who we are, and we look at how we might contribute to solving those problems.

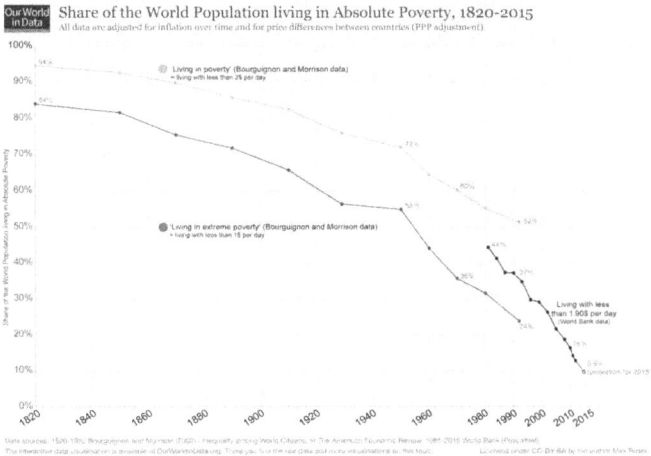

Share of the World Population living in Absolute Poverty, 1820-2015
All data are adjusted for inflation over time and for price differences between countries (PPP adjustment).

One of the great global problems, yet little discussed, is close to being resolved. Over the past two to three decades, we have seen a rapid decline in absolute poverty. Look at this chart. (See link to the article in Resources section.) Look at the drop in the percentage of the world that was living on $1.90 per day. It went from 45% to 9% in 35 years. Those numbers send chill up my spine.

I have been to villages that live on the margins of extreme poverty. To imagine what it took for this increase in human prosperity to occur, I know that there are millions of people who are working hard to solve this problem.

Some of these problem solvers are training people how to farm as an economic solution to their poverty. Others are building schools that equip students with math and reading skills. There are hospitals and public health programs that are contributing. Every endeavor contributes to the whole.

To be a problem solver, you don't start at the level of global poverty. Instead, you start with the problems that affect your neighbors. You already know what those problems are. They are the ones that you talk about at work or the corner deli. We are not at a loss to know where the problems are. We are at a loss in terms of the motivation to solve them.

What should be our motivation to solve the problems that affect our local communities? We can toss in words like compassion, empathy, or tired of waiting for someone else to do it.

However, the real motivation is that we can. We have within ourselves the capacity to solve every problem that crosses our attention span. This is where all that latent potential gets put to use.

Earlier I told the story of Emmanuel and his efforts to feed the people of his community in Uganda. He started by asking me for advice. He acted on that advice and succeeded. Success is a powerful motivator. Then, he grows maize and distributed it to his people. He'll do that again.

What will follow this? He is talking about buying a vacant lot near his church and building a building on it. He has plans. He isn't some wealthy entrepreneur. He is just a guy who is motivated to be a problem solver.

My advice to each of you is that you start the same way. Identify a problem that is primarily not about your personal situation. Start talking to people about how we could fix this problem.

Take the Circle of Impact and the Five Questions and used them to help frame a response to the problem that lets you take the first step. That is all. Just take the first step. Then, look back and see what you learned.

As you go through this process, take notes. Keep a journal. Start a blog where you write about what you are learning. Do something that allows you to reflect with depth on what you are doing, as well as, articulates a story that you can tell. Your story can invite others to join you. As they join you, agree with one another to act as a network of relationships. If you need help, contact me.

The Future of Problem Solving

In my book, Circle of Impact: Taking Personal Initiative To Ignite Change, I write about the Two Global Forces. There is the global force of centralized institutions of governance and finance.

And there is the global force of decentralized networks of relationships. During the COVID-19 pandemic, we have witnessed how the centralized force operates. For some people, they have learned how to create the networks of relationships. The real change is not in those that managed the pandemic. They were always there. Though their presence was not felt so significantly.

The creation and expansion of networks of relationships is new. It points to the future. Problem solving from a global centralized position operates with a one size fits all strategy. It is easy to control seven billion people when everyone must operate by the same rules.

The reality though is that we are not all the same. We are an incredibly diverse world that is now linked through digital communication technology that does not always require intermediary institutions to negotiate how we work together. The future is in the network.

When you create networks of relationships for problem solving you join a generation, not unlike that of Einstein and Curie. They were the vanguard of a scientific revolution that change human history forever. The facility of networking together to solve local problems I am convinced has a similar promise.

The future needs us to be problem solvers. Just start somewhere. Start with something small, and something local. Do something where you can see the impact that makes a difference that matters. This kind of change is a great motivator.

If you need help, email me at ed@edbrenegar.com, and we'll figure out what your next step is. Thank you for your future impact that will make a difference that matters.

References

Persons:

Niels Bohr - https://en.wikipedia.org/wiki/Niels_Bohr.

Marie Curie - https://en.wikipedia.org/wiki/Marie_Curie

Guy Debord - https://en.wikipedia.org/wiki/Guy_Debord

Paul Dirac - https://en.wikipedia.org/wiki/Paul_Dirac

Peter Drucker - https://en.wikipedia.org/wiki/Peter_Drucker

Albert Einstein - https://en.wikipedia.org/wiki/Albert_Einstein

Werner Eisenberg - https://en.wikipedia.org/wiki/Werner_Heisenberg

Rene' Girard - https://en.wikipedia.org/wiki/
Ren%C3%A9_Girard

Kurt Gödel - https://en.wikipedia.org/wiki/
Kurt_G%C3%B6del

Daniel Kahneman - https://en.wikipedia.org/wiki/
Daniel_Kahneman

Maurice Merleau- - https://en.wikipedia.org/wiki/
Maurice_Merleau-Ponty

Max Planck - https://en.wikipedia.org/wiki/
Max_Planck

Michael Polanyi - https://en.wikipedia.org/wiki/
Michael_Polanyi

Erwin Shrödinger - https://en.wikipedia.org/wiki/
Erwin_Schr%C3%B6dinger

History

President Kennedy's Go-to-the-Moon Speech –

Text - https://er.jsc.nasa.gov/seh/ricetalk.htm

Video - https://youtu.be/QAmHcdwKgtQ

Solvay Conference 1927

History - https://en.wikipedia.org/wiki/
Solvay_Conference

Group Portrait

https://www.daily-sun.com/assets/news_
images/2016/12/16/DailySun-2016-12-16-05-21.jpg

Drop in Extreme Poverty – Gapminder Foundation

https://www.gapminder.org/data/documentation/
epovrate/

Who is Dr. Ed Brenegar?

Dr. Ed Brenegar is a global thought leader, trainer, speaker, and networker. His purpose is to inspire and equip people world-wide to take personal initiative to create impact for their local communities. He has created the Circle of Impact Institute to expand his impact through his writing and training. He is the author of Circle of Impact: Taking Personal Initiative To Ignite Change. He is the Founder and Facilitator of the Global Impact Network whose purpose is the establishment and support local networks of relationships on a global scale.

Circle of Impact Institute:

Publications

> *Circle of Impact: Taking Personal Initiative to Ignite Change* Translations: English, Chinese (Mandarin), Arabic

> *Circle of Impact Africa* – English, French

21st Century Leadership Guide series

Leading For Impact weblog – https://edbrenegar.com/blog

Training

Impact Day Consultation - Planning / Problem Solving for Individuals and Groups

Circle of Impact Introduction Video Series - Free

Advanced Circle of Impact Training Video Series – Fee-based

Global Impact Network:

Network of Relationships Training

Facilitation for Formation and Development of local networks for impact

Contact Information:

Dr. Ed Brenegar
Circle of Impact, LLC.
ed@edbrenegar.com
+1-828-275-1803
https://edbrenegar.com

www.ingramcontent.com/pod-product-compliance
Lightning Source LLC
Chambersburg PA
CBHW070816050426
42452CB00011B/2069